Nutrias Invade Marshes and Waterways

By Susan H. Gray

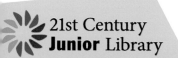

21st Century
Junior Library

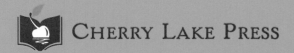
CHERRY LAKE PRESS

Published in the United States of America by Cherry Lake Publishing Group
Ann Arbor, Michigan
www.cherrylakepublishing.com

Reading Adviser: Beth Walker Gambro, MS, Ed., Reading Consultant, Yorkville, IL
Book Designer: Melinda Millward

Photo Credits: © Firn/Shutterstock.com, cover; © Ondrej Prosicky/Shutterstock.com, 4;
© Nikola Cedikova/Shutterstock.com, 6; © Dan Campbell/Shutterstock.com, 8; © U. Eisenlohr/
Shutterstock.com, 10; © Firn/Shutterstock.com, 12; © A Periam Photography/Shutterstock.com,
14; © Kim Miller Media/Shutterstock.com, 16; © Courtesy of the USDA Wildlife Services, 18;
© SanderMeertinsPhotography/Shutterstock.com, 20

Cherry Lake Press is an imprint of Cherry Lake Publishing Group.
Library of Congress Cataloging-in-Publication Data

Names: Gray, Susan Heinrichs, author.
Title: Nutrias invade marshes and waterways / by Susan H. Gray.
Description: Ann Arbor, Michigan : Cherry Lake Publishing, 2021. | Series:
    Invasive species science : tracking and controlling | Includes index. | Audience: Grades 2-3
Identifiers: LCCN 2021004902 (print) | LCCN 2021004903 (ebook) | ISBN 9781534187016
    (hardcover) | ISBN 9781534188419 (paperback) | ISBN 9781534189812 (pdf) |
    ISBN 9781534191211 (ebook)
Subjects: LCSH: Coypu—Control—United States—Juvenile literature. | Introduced animals—United
    States—Juvenile literature. | Invasive species—Control—United States—Juvenile literature.
Classification: LCC QL737.R668 G73 2021 (print) | LCC QL737.R668 (ebook) |
    DDC 599.35/90973—dc23
LC record available at https://lccn.loc.gov/2021004902
LC ebook record available at https://lccn.loc.gov/2021004903

Cherry Lake Publishing Group would like to acknowledge the work of the Partnership for 21st
Century Learning, a Network of Battelle for Kids. Please visit http://www.battelleforkids.org/
networks/p21 for more information.

Printed in the United States of America
Corporate Graphics

CONTENTS

Nutrias live along lakes, marshes, and streams.

Nutrias Take Over

"Good dog!" Marnie praised her **canine** partner. Keeva had discovered signs of a **nutria** nearby. Marnie and Keeva were checking out a **marsh** in Maryland.

Think!

Nutrias often eat the entire root system of a plant. Why is this worse than just eating the stems and leaves?

Nutrias eat up to one-fourth of their weight in plants each day.

Nutrias are **rodents**. They burrow into banks and create their own tunnel systems.

At first, these animals lived only in South America. But things began to change in the late 1800s. That's when people everywhere discovered the nutria's luxurious coat. Soon, a demand for nutria jackets and hats arose. North Americans, Europeans, and Asians began to **import** the animals. They planned to raise nutrias for their fur. At the time, no one realized what a mistake that was.

Nutrias are social and will sometimes live in groups.

Coming to America

In the United States, nutrias were great for the fur industry. Plus, an **invasive** weed was blocking up rivers and streams. Surely, some hungry nutrias could get it under control.

People soon learned the truth. Like the weeds, nutrias were invasive. They escaped into the wild and had few **predators**. And they totally failed to control the invasive weed.

Nutrias have orange-colored teeth.

In the 1980s, fur coats became less popular. But by this time, nutrias already inhabited much of the southern United States.

The animals were also in Maryland and several other states. Once they moved in, they destroyed the natural plant life. Next, the birds, fish, crabs, and other wildlife disappeared.

Make a Guess!

In Louisiana, nutrias have tunneled into **levees**. Levees are often made of soil. They block flood waters from rushing in. How would tunnels affect a levee's strength?

Nutrias are semiaquatic, meaning they spend
time on land and in the water.

Different Places, Different Plans

Scientists began working on ways to control the invaders. But first, they had to answer many questions.

The first step was to find all the places where nutrias lived. So wildlife experts searched waterways for signs. They looked for burrows dug into riverbanks. They looked for tender plants with their tips chewed off. They even looked for nutria **scat**.

While at first glance, nutrias may look similar to beavers, their tails are long and round instead of flat.

Such studies showed just how big the nutria problem was. There was no way to remove them. The best solution was to keep their numbers under control.

Now, the state pays trappers for each nutria they catch. Alligators in Louisiana also play a role. They are among the few nutria predators. The rodents make up a major part of their diet.

Ask Questions!

Some people thought it would be a good idea to poison the nutrias. How might this affect other animals?

Hunting dogs are trained to identify nutria scat.

Scientists in Maryland had a different approach. Their nutria problem was in Chesapeake Bay. The bay is a large area where Maryland's rivers flow into the sea. Experts in Maryland decided to **eradicate** the nutrias there.

At first, the experts used traps. This helped, but it was not enough. Next, they used hunting dogs. They would sniff out nutrias and howl when they found them. This method also helped, but some nutrias still remained. It was time to bring in some very special dogs.

Keeva retired in 2017 and was adopted by Marnie.

Keeva and Marnie

Scientists chose dogs that were very smart and full of energy. They sent the dogs to a school in Georgia for training. There, they learned to follow commands and work with a handler.

These dogs combed through Chesapeake Bay. Now, only a few hundred nutrias remain. Keeva was one of those chosen dogs, and Marnie was her handler.

A nutria is also called a coypu.

In Louisiana and in Maryland, the programs continue. The Louisiana program uses trappers. The Maryland program keeps watching for nutrias. Other states have their own efforts. Scientists around the country share what they've learned about nutria control. Perhaps one day, these invaders will no longer be a problem.

Look!

Find pictures online of nutrias. What can you tell about their lives just by looking at their photos?

GLOSSARY

canine (KAY-nine) having to do with dogs

eradicate (ee-RAD-ih-kayt) to completely remove

import (im-PORT) to bring in from another place

invasive (in-VAY-sihv) not native, but entering by force or by accident and spreading quickly

levees (LEH-veez) ridges, usually of earth, that run alongside rivers to hold back flood waters

marsh (MARSH) a low, wet land, often flooded, and having grasses and cattails

nutria (NOO-tree-uh) a large rodent similar to a beaver

predators (PRED-uh-turz) animals that hunt and eat other animals

rodents (ROH-duhnts) an animal group including mice and rats, that have fur

scat (SKAT) the droppings left by a wild animal

FIND OUT MORE

BOOKS

Gilles, Renae. *Invasive Species in Infographics*. Ann Arbor, MI: Cherry Lake Publishing, 2020.

O'Connor, Karen. *The Threat of Invasive Species*. New York, NY: Gareth Stevens Publishing, 2014.

Spilsbury, Richard. *Invasive Mammal Species*. New York, NY: PowerKids Press, 2015.

WEBSITES

Cool Green Science—Recovery by Eradication: Saving Marshes from Nutria
https://blog.nature.org/science/2018/08/21/recovery-by-eradication-saving-marshes-from-nutria
Scroll through this article to see great pictures of nutria, marshes before and after recovery, and the real Marnie and Keeva.

Enchanted Learning—Nutria (Coypu)
https://www.enchantedlearning.com/subjects/mammals/rodent/Nutria.shtml
Learn about the nutria's habits and its predators.

SoftSchools—Nutria Facts
https://www.softschools.com/facts/animals/nutria_facts/489/
This site has a whole list of nutria fun facts.

INDEX

ABOUT THE AUTHOR

Susan H. Gray has a master's degree in zoology. She has written more than 180 reference books for children and especially loves writing about animals. Susan lives in Cabot, Arkansas, with her husband, Michael, and many pets.